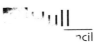 

# Nutty Nonsense

Author and Illustrator: Colin West

## A few words from Colin West: ...

When I learned of Christina's charity, Children's Literature Festivals, I was very happy to help by compiling a book of my most popular poems and adding new illustrations. Some of my most treasured memories are of the letters or emails I've received over the years from children who have told me that my books have helped them to enjoy reading. One or two have even become successful writers themselves!

To see and hear authors performing their work is something a child will always remember, and the writers Christina gathers for events are truly inspiring.

To reach lots of children and show them the fun that books can bring can only be a good thing. Long may Children's Literature Festivals thrive!

Thanks to Christina for assisting with this project.

**Author and Illustrator: Colin West**
**copyright of poems and illustrations Colin West**

**Published by Poems & Pictures Publishing © 2022**

**ISBN: 9781739835590**

A CIP catalogues record of the publication is available from the British Library:

Proceeds from book sales to Children's Literature Festivals charity: 1182143 England & Wales

Special thanks to Martin Holmes and Editor Rebecca Thomas

# Contents

# Introduction

Here are rhymes to read to others:
Fathers, mothers, sisters, brothers.
Here are poems in their dozens
For your grannies and your cousins.
Here are tales of crazy creatures
To be read to friends and teachers.
Here are songs and here are shanties
For your uncles and your aunties.
And in this book upon your shelf
Are words to keep just for yourself.

7

# Moose

What use
a moose?
Except, perhaps
for coats and caps.

# Norman Norton's Nostrils

O, Norman Norton's nostrils
Are powerful and strong,
Hold on to your belongings
If he should come along.

And do not ever let him
Inhale with all his might,
Or else your pens and pencils
Will disappear from sight.

Right up his nose they'll vanish,
Your future will look black.
Unless he gets the sneezes,
You'll *never* get them back!

# My Sister Sybil

Sipping soup, my sister Sybil
Seems inclined to drool and dribble.
If it wasn't for this foible,
Mealtimes would be more enjoible.

# Joe

We don't mention Joe
In this house any more.
No, not since he nailed
Granny's boots to the floor.
What makes matters worse
With regard to the crime
Is Granny was wearing
Her boots at the time.

# Don't Look in the Mirror, Maud

O don't look in the mirror, Maud,
I fear that you might crack it,
A new one I could not afford,
Unless I sold my jacket.

And if I sold my jacket, Maud,
I could no longer wear it,
And then I couldn't go abroad,
I'm sure I couldn't bear it

For if I couldn't travel, Maud,
I'd never get to Venice,
I'd have to stay behind with Claud,
And practise playing tennis.

And if he were to ask me, Maud,
If we could play mixed doubles,
He'd thereby contribute toward
My many other troubles.

For if we played mixed doubles, Maud,
With Vivienne and Vera,
They'd brush their long hair afterward
Before that very mirror.

And if 'twere broke,
   they'd be appalled,
And hit me with my
   racket,
So don't look in the
   mirror, Maud,
I fear that you might
   crack it.

# Some Tongue-twisters

When Jilly eats jelly,
Then Jilly is jolly,
But melons make Melanie
Most melancholy.

Adelaide is up a ladder.
Adelaide's an adder-upper.
She's an addled adder-upper,
Adding adders up a ladder.

To begin to toboggan, first buy a toboggan,
But don't buy too big a toboggan.
A too big a toboggan is not a toboggan
To buy to begin to toboggan.

I can't canoe my old canoe,
I need a new canoe.
Can you canoe my old canoe,
And I'll canoe the new?

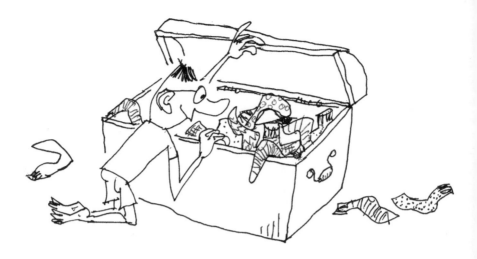

# My Socks

I have a great big laundry box
And stuffed inside are all my socks:
Black socks, white socks,
Morning, noon and night socks,
Grey socks, green socks,
Small, large and in-between socks,
Blue socks, brown socks,
Always-falling-down socks,
Orange socks, red socks,
Baby socks and bed socks,
Purple socks, pink socks,
What-would-people-think socks,
Long socks, short socks,
Every-sort-of-sport socks,

Saggy socks, tight socks,
Snazzy far-too-bright socks,
Holey socks, frayed socks,
Very badly made socks,
Chequered socks, tartan socks,
School or kindergarten socks,
Sensible socks, silly socks,
Frivolous and frilly socks,
Impractical socks, impossible socks,
Drip-dry, machine-only-washable socks,
Sicilian socks, Brazilian socks,
There seem to be over a *million* socks!

With all these socks, there's just one catch —
It's hard to find a pair that match.

# Little Barbara

Little Barbara went to Scarborough,
Just to buy a candelabra.
At the harbour a bear ate Barbara.
Don't you find that most macabre?

# An Understanding Man

I have an understanding
With an understanding man:
His umbrella I stand under
When I understand I can.

# Passersby

A passerby was
Passing by a bypass,
And passing by the bypass
A passerby passed by.
By passing by a bypass
As a passerby passed by,
A passerby was passed by
By a bypass passerby.

# The Cat and the King

A cat may look at a king
And a king may look at a cat.
If thin the cat and fat the king,
There isn't much danger in that.
But just suppose fat is the cat,
Conversely, thin the king.
The king gets mighty cross at that,
And stamps like anything.

# Barge Pole

Poetry?
I wouldn't touch it with a barge pole.

Well,
How about:
A long pole,
A lean pole,
A bamboo or
A bean pole?
A flag pole,
A tent pole,
A barber's or
A bent pole?
A green pole,
A grey pole,
A curtain or
A maypole?
A whole pole,
A half pole,
A great big
Telegraph pole?

No!
Not any sort.
No small pole,
No large pole,
I wouldn't touch it with a barge pole!

# My Uncle is a Baronet

My uncle is a baronet,
He sleeps beside the hearth,
And likes to play the clarinet
When sitting in the bath.

# She Likes to Swim

She likes to swim beneath the sea
And wear her rubber flippers.
She likes to dance outrageously
And wake up all the kippers.

# The Orang-Utan

The closest relative of man,
They say, is the orang-utan.
And when I look at Grandpapa,
I realise how right they are!

23

# Jingle-Jangle-Jent

A Viking liking hiking walked
From Kathmandu to Kent,
And Timbuktu and Teddington
Were towns he did frequent.
And yet with everything he saw
And everywhere he went,
He never ever saw the sight
Of Jingle-Jangle-Jent.
He *never* ever saw the sight
Of Jingle-Jangle-Jent.

A Druid fond of fluid drank
More than you've ever dreamt.
It took a dozen pints of ale
Until he was content.
And yet with all the liquid that
He to his tummy sent,
He never ever knew the taste
Of Jingle-Jangle-Jent,
He *never* ever knew the taste
Of Jingle-Jangle-Jent.

A vet whose pet was prone to fret
In Ancient Egypt spent
His life with sickly squeaks and
   squeals,
To which his ears he lent.
He learnt what every whimper was,
What every mumble meant,
And yet he never heard the noise
Of Jingle-Jangle-Jent,
He *never* ever heard the noise
Of Jingle-Jangle-Jent.

A Roman roamin' round in Rome
Aromas did invent,
By mixing potions in a pot,
As over it he bent.
His nostrils were of noble nose,
Yet it is evident,
He never ever caught the whiff
Of Jingle-Jangle-Jent,
He *never* ever caught the whiff
Of Jingle-Jangle-Jent.

# Adolphus

Adolphus is despicable,
Before the day begins
To prove that I am kickable,
He kicks me in the shins.

# The Trouble with Boys

The trouble with boys is
They make funny noises.
They rage and they riot
And seldom are quiet.
They seem extra naughty
With folk over forty,
And do things they oughtn't
To persons important.

# Trampoline

I'm sorry to disturb you, miss, I hate to intervene,

But could you for a moment, please, put down your magazine?

I've got a hundred pounds to spend, and I am really keen,

If you could only serve me, miss, to buy this trampoline.

# An Alphabet of Horrible Habits

**A** is for Albert
who makes
lots of noise.

**B** is for Bertha
who bashes
the boys.

**C** is for Cuthbert
who teases
the cat.

**D** is for Dilys
whose singing
is flat.

**E** is for Enid
who's never
on time.

**F** is for Freddie
who's covered
in slime.

**G** is for Gilbert
who never
says thanks.

**H** is for Hannah
who plans  to
rob banks.

**I** is for Ivy
who slams
every door.

**J** is for Jacob
whose jokes
are a bore.

**K** is for Kenneth
who won't wash
his face.

**L** is for Lucy
who cheats
in a race.

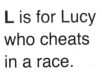

**M** is for Maurice
who gobbles
his food.

29

**N** is for Norma
whose manners
are rude.

**O** is for Olive
who treads
on your toes.

**P** is for Percy
who *will* pick
his nose.

**Q** is for Queenie
who won't tell
the truth.

**R** is for Rupert
who's rather
uncouth.

**S** is for Sibyl
who bellows
and bawls.

**T** is for Thomas
who scribbles
on walls.

**U** is for Una
who fidgets
too much.

**V** is for Victor
who talks
double Dutch.

**W** is for Wilma
who won't wipe
her feet.

**X** is for Xander
who never
is neat.

**Y** is for Yorik
who's vain
as can be.

And **Z** is for Zoe
who doesn't
love me.

# When Rover Passed Over

When Rover died, my sister cried,
I tried my best to calm her.
I said, "We'll have him mummified,
I know a good embalmer."

And so we packed the wretched pup
Into a wicker basket,
And duly had him bandaged up,
And kept him in a casket.

Now Rover we will not forget,
Though he is but a dummy,
For though we've lost a faithful pet,
We've gained an extra mummy!

# The Bridle and the Saddle

The bridle and the saddle
Fitted, I sit in the middle
Of the horse, but why I straddle
Such a creature is a riddle.

O, he's big and I am little,
And he no doubt thinks I'm idle,
And he knows my bones be brittle
As I hang on to the bridle.

But it doesn't seem to addle
Him that I am in a muddle,
As I cower in the saddle
When we pass over each puddle.

# Me and Amanda

Me
  and
    Amanda
       meander,
      like
      rivers
    that
      run
        to
         the
           sea.

        We
          wander
            at
              random,
                we're
                  always
                  in
                tandem,
                meandering
            Mandy
          and
        me!

# Park Regulations

The rules upon this board displayed
Are here for all to be obeyed:

Keep off the grass. Don't scale the wall.
Don't throw, or kick, or bat a ball.
Don't pluck the flowers from their bed.
Don't feed the ducks with crusts of bread.
Bicycles may not be ridden.
Rollerskating is forbidden.
Dogs must be kept upon their leashes
And kept from chasing other species.
Dispose of litter thoughtfully.
Do not attempt to climb a tree,
And don't build fires or gather sticks.
The gates are closed at half past six.

Observe these rules and regulations.
(Signed) Head of Parks and Recreations.

# Old Shivermetimbers

Old Shivermetimbers, the sea-faring cat,
Was born on the edge of the ocean,
And his days (just to prove that the world isn't flat)
Are spent in perpetual motion.

Old Shivermetimbers, the nautical cat,
Has seen every port of the atlas,
First feline he was, to set foot in Rabat,
A place which was hitherto catless.

Old Shivermetimbers, the sea-faring cat,
Has numbered as seventy-seven
The times that he's chartered the cold Kattegat
And steered by the stars up in Heaven.

Old Shivermetimbers, the nautical cat,
Loves the scent of the sea on his whiskers,
So it isn't surprising to hear him say that
He don't give a hoot for hibiscus.

Old Shivermetimbers, the sea-faring cat,
Has travelled aboard the *Queen Mary*,
Though I saw him last Saturday queuing up at
Calais, for the cross-Channel ferry.

Old Shivermetimbers, the nautical cat,
Has spent his whole life on the ocean,
Yet how he acquired that old admiral's hat,
I honestly haven't a notion.

# In Other Words

Dare we watch a scary movie
All about a monster menace?
Then, maybe you'd care to join me
In a game of table tennis?
Later I may serenade you
Like the gondoliers of Venice.
In other words …

Let's watch King Kong,
Have a ding dong

Game of ping pong
And a sing song.

# The Lighthouse Keeper

I met the lighthouse
  keeper's wife,
His nephew, niece
  and daughter,
His uncle and his
  auntie too,
When I went across
  the water.

I met the lighthouse
  keeper's son,
His father and his
  mother,
His grandpa and his
  grandma too,
His sister and his
  brother.

I met the lighthouse
  keeper's mate,
Who, running out
  of patience,
Told me, "The keeper's
  gone ashore
To round up more
  relations!"

39

# George Washington

George Washington chopped down a tree
And couldn't tell a lie.
When questioned by his father, he
Confessed, "Yes, it was I."

But as he handed in the axe,
He added in defence,
"Good training, sir, for lumberjacks
Or would-be presidents."

# Raleigh and Elizabeth

When Raleigh met Elizabeth
And it was rather muddy,
He wouldn't let her feet get wet,
He *was* a fuddy-duddy.

So he laid down his velvet cloak,
The Queen, she didn't falter.
She thought it odd, but on it trod,
And said, "Arise, Sir Walter."

# Auntie Agnes's Cat

My Auntie Agnes has a cat,
I do not like to tell her that
Its body seems a little large,
With lots of stripes for camouflage.
Its teeth and claws are also larger
Than they ought to be. A rajah
Gave her the kitten, I recall,
When she was stationed in Bengal.
But that was many years ago,
And kittens are inclined to grow,
So now she has a fearsome cat,
But I don't like to tell her that.

# The Loofah

The loofah feels
  he can't relax,
For something
  is amiss:
He scratches other
  people's backs,
But no one
  scratches *his*.

# Fungus

It's most fantastic fun to be a fungus,
But no one seems to care for us a lot,
So for revenge, the mischievous among us
Look edible, but actually are not.

# Our Hippopotamus

We thought a lively pet to keep
Might be a hippopotamus.
Now see him sitting in a heap
And notice at the bottom, us!

# Glowworm

I know a worried glowworm,
I wonder what the matter is?
He seems so glum and gloomy,
Perhaps he needs new batteries!

# The Tortoise

The tortoise has a tendency
To live beyond his prime,
Thus letting his descendants see
How *they* will look in time.

# French Accents

Acute, or Grave or Circumflex,
In France we use all three,
And sometimes too, Cedilla who
Is found beneath the C.

# Ben

Ben's done something really bad,
He's forged a letter from his dad …

Dear Miss Mc.Kee
Please let Ben be
excused this week from all
P.E.
He has a bad cold in his chest
and so I think it might be
best
if he throughout this week
could be
excused from doing all P.E.
I hope my writing's not
too bad.
Yours sincerely
signed Ben's Dad.
XXXXX

# Have You Ever?

Have
you
ever
perched
a
poem
on
your
nose?

Have you
ever worn
a ditty
on your
clothes?

Have you ever sniffed a sonnet in a rose?

# Knitting

She tried to knit a nightcap,
She tried to knit a scarf,
She tried to knit a cardigan,
Too big they were, by half.

She tried to knit a waistcoat,
She tried to knit a shawl,
She tried to knit a bobble hat,
They all turned out too small.

And now she's knitting knickers,
And if *they* do not fit.
We'll make her wear them anyhow.
Until she's learnt to knit.

# Muddled Words

O, Longitude and Latitude,
I always get them muddled.
I'm sure they'd be offended,
   though,
To think that I'm befuddled.

O, Isobars and Isotherms,
Please tell me how they differ,
For competition 'twixt
   the two,
I hear, could not be stiffer.

O, Stalagmites and Stalactites,
Whenever I peruse 'em,
Though one grows up, and one
   grows down,
I can't help but confuse 'em.

# The Pig

The table manners of the pig
Leave much to be desired,
His appetite is always big,
His talk is uninspired.

And if you ask him out to dine,
You'll only ask him once,
Unless you like to see a swine
Who gobbles as he grunts.

# The Darkest and Dingiest Dungeon

Down in the darkest and dingiest dungeon,
Far from the tiniest twinkle of stars,
Far from the whiff of a wonderful luncheon,
Far from the murmur of motoring cars,
Far from the habits of rabbits and weasels,
Far from the merits of ferrets and stoats,
Far from the danger of mumps or of measles,
Far from the fashions of fabulous coats,
Far from the turn of a screw in a socket,
Far from the fresh frozen food in the fridge,
Far from the fluff in my duffle coat pocket,
Far from the bite of a mischievous midge,
Far from the hole in my humble umbrella,
Far from my hat as it hangs in the hall,
I sit here alone with myself in the cellar,
I *do* so like getting away from it all!

# U.F.O.

A UFO, a UFO,
have you ever
seen a UFO?

Yes, I've seen a UFO —
an Ugly Frog Ogling
a rather pretty crow.

A UFO, a UFO,
have you ever
seen a UFO?

Yes, I've seen a UFO —
an Uncouth Fellow, Oswald,
not very nice to know.

A UFO, a UFO,
have you ever
seen a UFO?

Yes, I've seen a UFO —
an Ultra Friendly Ox
showed me the way to go.

A UFO, a UFO,
have you ever
seen a UFO?

Yes, I've seen a UFO —
an Understanding Freckled Owl,
whose voice was soft and low.

A UFO, a UFO,
have you ever
seen a UFO?

Yes, I've seen a UFO —
an Unbelieving Foolish Oaf
I met not long ago.

A UFO, a UFO,
you've never seen
a UFO!

But I have, I'll let you know —
my Unique Flying Object
awaits me, cheerio!

# Custard

I like it thin without a skin,
My sister likes it thicker.
But thick or thin, when tucking in,
I'm noisier and quicker!

# When Betty Eats Spaghetti

When Betty eats spaghetti,
She slurps, she slurps, she slurps,
And when she's finished slurping,
She burps, she burps, she burps.

# Pogo Stick

Upon my pogo stick I pounce
And out of school I homeward bounce.
I bounce so high, how my heart pounds
Until at last I'm out of bounds.

# The Saddest Spook

The saddest spook there ever was
Is melancholy just because
He can't so much as raise a sneer
Or laugh a laugh that's vaguely queer.
He hasn't learned to walk through walls,
And dares not answer wolfish calls,
And when big ghosts are rude and coarse,
And shout at him, "Your fangs are false!"
He smiles at them just like a fool,
But wishes they'd pick on a ghoul
Who's heavyweight and not just bantam,
*Why* pick on a little phantom?

# Dressing Gown

Why do people I'm
   addressing frown
When I've got on my
   dressing gown?
And some give me
   a dressing down
When I've got on my
   dressing gown?

# Bed of Nails

I sleep upon a bed of nails,
I must confess it never fails
To help me get a good night's rest,
And over all, I'm most impressed!

# My Auntie

My auntie who lives in
Llanfairpwllgwyngyllgogerych-
    wyrndrobwillllantysiliogogogoch
Has asked me to stay.

But unfortunately
Llanfairpwllgwyngyllgogerych-
    wyrndrobwillllantysiliogogogoch
Is a long, long way away.

Will I ever go to
Llanfairpwllgwyngwllgogerych-
    wyrndrobwillllantysiliogogogoch?
It's difficult to say.

# Mr Lott's Allotment

Mr Lott's allotment
Meant a lot to Mr Lott.
Now Mr Lott is missed a lot
On Mr Lott's allotment.

# What do Teachers Dream of?

What do teachers dream of
In mountains and in lowlands?
They dream of exclamation marks,
Full stops and semicolons!

# Orange Silver Sausage

Some words I've studied for a time,
Like *orange, silver, sausage,*
But as for finding them a rhyme,
I'm at a total lossage.

# Juggler Jim

I'm Jim and I juggle a jug and a jar,
And junkets and jelly and jam.
With jovial, joyful and jocular jests,
How jolly a jester I am!

# Rolling Down a Hill

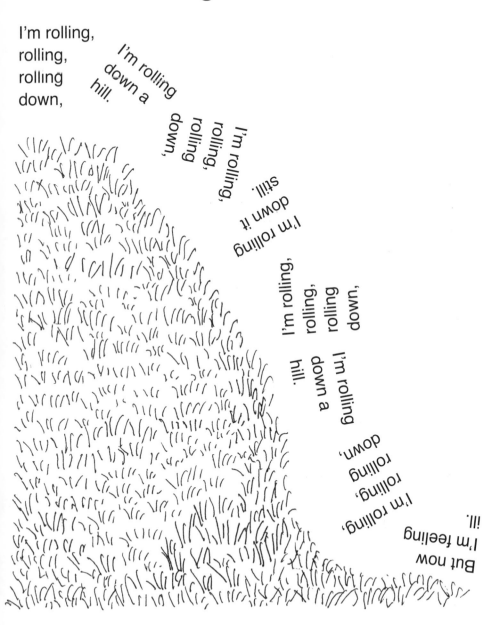

I'm rolling,
rolling,
rolling
down,

I'm rolling
down a
hill.

I'm rolling,
rolling,
rolling
down,

I'm rolling,
rolling,
still.

I'm rolling
down it
still.

I'm rolling,
rolling,
rolling
down,

I'm rolling
down a
hill.

I'm rolling,
rolling,
rolling
down,

But now
I'm feeling
ill.

# The Prize Pumpkin

They seized it, they squeezed it,
They gave it funny looks,
They teased it, they eased it,
They looked it up in books.
They tethered it, they weathered it,
Then realised they treasured it,
And when they could, they measured it,
(It came to seven foot).

> They gave it a prod,
> They gave it a poke,
> They sang it a song,
> And told it a joke.

They ran to it, they walked to it,
They then began to talk to it,
They lathered it, (they rathered it
Was shiny as could be).
They smothered it, they mothered it,
They fathered and they brothered it,
They watered it, they daughtered it,
And hugged it lovingly.

They gave it a pinch,
They gave it a punch,
They cut it in bits
And had it for lunch!

# Proboscis Monkey

Proboscis Monkey, I suppose
You've grown accustomed to
   your nose,
But what precisely did you do
To get that nose to grow on you?

# Anteater

Hey, have you met my nice new pet?
An anteater is he!
There's just one hitch — I'm apt to itch
When serving up his tea.

# Geraldine Giraffe

The
longest
ever
woolly
scarf
was
worn
by
Geraldine
Giraffe.
Around
her
neck
the
scarf
she
wound,
but
still
it
trailed
upon
the
ground.

# Aunt Carol

Making vinegar, Aunt Carol
Fell into her brimming barrel.
As she drowned, my teardrops
  trickled:
Now she's permanently
  pickled!

# Laurence

Laurence by a lion was mauled,
And it's left us quite appalled.
He had on his Sunday Best,
Now he's gone and torn his vest.

# The Blunderblat

Until I saw the Blunderblat
I doubted its existence,
But late last night with
   Vera White
I saw one in the distance.

I reached for my binoculars,
Which finally I focused,
And watched it rise into
   the skies
Like some colossal locust.

I heard it hover overhead,
I shrieked as it came nearer,
I held my breath, half scared
   to death,
And prayed it might take Vera.

And so it did, I'm glad to say,
Without too much resistance.
Dear Blunderblat, I'm sorry
   that
I doubted your existence.

# A Pelican in Delhi Can

A pelican in Delhi can
Spend his whole life alone.
But an elephant in Delhi can't
Be often on his own.

70

# Uncle Harry

My Uncle Harry
had a horse,

But kept on
falling off it.

We charged a
pound to come
and watch,

And made a
handsome profit.

# Clumsy Clarissa

Clarissa did the washing up:
She smashed a plate and chipped a cup,
And dropped a glass and cracked a mug,
Then pulled the handle off a jug.
She couldn't do much worse, you'd think,
But then she went and broke the sink.

# Putting the Shot

Tomorrow I may put the shot,
Or on the other hand, may not.
For yesterday I put the shot,
But where I put it, I forgot.

# Wobble-dee-woo

What would you do
With a Wobble-dee-woo?
Would you eat it
Or wear it or play it?
What would you do
With a  Wobble-dee-woo?
I've only just learned
How to say it.

What would you do
With a Wobble-dee-woo?
Would you wear it
Or play it or eat it?
What would you do
With a Wobble-dee-woo?
I'm sorry, I'll have
To repeat it …

What would you do
With a Wobble-dee-woo?
Would you play it
Or eat it or wear it?
What would you do
With a Wobble-dee-woo?
It's driving me mad,
I can't bear it!

# Octopus

Last Saturday I came across
Most nonchalant an octopus.
I couldn't help but make a fuss
And shook him by the tentacle.

He seemed to find it all a bore
And asked me, "Have we met before?
I'm sorry, but I can't be sure,
You chaps all look identical."

# Veronica

Adventurous Veronica
Upon her yacht *Japonica*
Is sailing to Dominica.
She blows her old harmonica
Each night beneath the spinnaker
And dreams of seeing Monica,
Her sister, in Dominica.

# Auntie Dotty

Our Auntie Dotty thought it nice
To twirl about upon the ice.
We warned her persons of proportions
Such as hers, should take precautions.
But poor Aunt Dotty was so fond
Of skating on the village pond
That she took no heed of warning
And went skating one fine morning.

Now we mourn for Auntie Dot:
The ice was thin, but she was not.

# Annie and her Anaconda

Annie and her anaconda
Wander near and wander yonder.
When they wander here, I wonder
Whether Annie's anaconda
Likes it here, or is he fonder
Of the far-off places yonder?
(Where I wish I were, I ponder),
Excuse me while I grab my Honda!

# Nut Pickers

Who nicked the nuts
That the nut pickers picked
When the nut pickers
Picked their nuts?

The picnickers nicked
The nut pickers' nuts
When the nut pickers
Picked their nuts.

# Hither and Thither

Hither and thither
She plays on the zither,
Her music is ever so mellow.
But don't stop and dither,
Just look who is with her —
Her husband, who's playing
   the cello.

He scratches and screeches,
The high notes he reaches
Sound more like a cat being sat on.
Conductors throw peaches
When passing, and each is
Soon seen to be breaking his baton.

Both crotchet and quaver
Seem somehow to savour
A key neither major nor minor,
And if I were braver,
I'd ask him a favour,
"Why *don't* you please
   practise in China?"

# A Survey of Sovereigns

William, William, Henry the First,
Stephen and Henry the Second …

… Richard and John, sir, and Henry the Third,
Then one, two, three Edwards 'tis reckoned.

Richard the Second and Henry the Fourth,
And Henrys the Fifth and the Sixth, sir …

… Edward the Fourth and young Edward the Fifth,
Then Richard or Wicked King Dick, sir.

Henry the Seventh and Henry the Eighth,
Then Edward, then Mary was queen, sir …

… Elizabeth, James, then Kings Charles One and Two,
With Oliver Cromwell between, sir.

James, William & Mary, then following Anne,
Four Georges, one after another …

… Then William, Victoria, Edward and George,
To Edward, who said, "Crown my brother."

# Amongst my Friends

Amongst my friends, I number some
Sixteen or so who dance.
Some like to do the rhumba, some
Will waltz if they've the chance,
And even in their slumber, some
Will foxtrot in a trance,
But as for me, I'm cumbersome,
And all I do is prance.

## Jocelyn, my Dragon

My dragon's name is Jocelyn,
He's something of a joke,
For Jocelyn is very tame,
He doesn't like to maul or maim,
Or breathe a fearsome fiery flame —
He's much too smart to smoke.

And when I take him to the park,
The children form a queue,
And say, "What lovely eyes of red!"
As one by one they pat his head,
And Jocelyn is so well-bred,
He only eats a few!

# The Flipper-Flopper Bird

O have you never ever heard
Of the Flipper-Flopper Bird?
O have you never seen his teeth,
Two above and one beneath?

O have you never known the thrill
Of stroking his enormous bill?
O have you never taken tea
With him sitting up a tree?

O have you never seen him hop
As he goes a-flip, a-flop?
O have you never heard his cry?
No you've never? Nor have I.

# The Ogglewop

The Ogglewop is tall and wide,
And though he looks quite passive,
He's crammed with boys and girls inside —
That's why he is so massive!

# My Sister is Missing

Harriet, Harriet, jump on your chariot,
My sister is missing, poor Janet!
And Michael, O Michael, go pedal your cycle,
And search every part of the planet.
My sister, my sister, since breakfast I've missed her,
I'll never grow used to the silence.
So Cecil, O Cecil, I'm glad you can wrestle,
For Janet is prone to use violence.
With Doris and Maurice and Horace and Chloris
We'll follow the points of the compass,
And if we should find her, we'll creep up behind her,
But quietly, for Janet might thump us.

We'll hold her and scold her until we have told her
That running away isn't funny.
But if she says sorry, we'll hire a big lorry
And drive off to somewhere that's sunny.
We'll wander and ponder in fields over yonder,
But wait! What's that dot in the distance?
It looks like a figure, it's getting much bigger,
It's shouting at all my assistants!
O Janet, my Janet, it can't be, or can it?
My sister is no longer missing!
Hooray! We have found her, let's gather around her,
Let's start all the hugging and kissing!

# Insides

I'm very grateful for my skin
For keeping all my insides in.
I do so hate to think about
What I might look like inside-out.

# Kate

In the kitchen Kate went tripping,
Landing in a vat of dripping.
When the Red Cross came to fetch her,
Kate kept slipping off the stretcher.

# Kitty

Isn't it a
   dreadful pity
What became of
   dreamy Kitty,
Noticing the moon
   above her,
Not the missing
   man-hole cover?

# Betty

Wearing all her baubles, Betty
Rode too fast along the jetty.
How I wish she'd not been reckless —
We could not retrieve her necklace.

# Sports

Playing tennis
I'm no menace,
As for croquet,
I'm just "OK".
Then there's cricket:
Can't quite lick it,
Ditto: rowing,
Discus throwing,
Also: biking,
Jogging, hiking,
Ten-pin bowling
And pot-holing.
Can't play hockey.
I'm no jockey.
Daren't go riding
Or hang-gliding,
Nor can I  jump
Long or high jump.
Being sporty
Ain't my forté.
I'm pathetic,
Non-athletic,
But at dinner
I'm a winner!

# Hedgehog's Valentine

If you're sickly,
Feeling prickly,
As your trickly
Tears fall thickly,
Don't act fickly,
Kiss me quickly,
You'll feel tickly,
Not so prickly,
And partickly
Far from sickly.

# Willoughby

I want to be a wallaby,
A wallaby like Willoughby.
When *will* I be a wallaby
Like Willoughby the wallaby?

(To read this poem, be like Tom and start at the bottom and work your way up!

# Tom

Divinity.
a Doctor of
and was soon
He spoke with angels
Infinity:
and vanished in
one afternoon
Tom climbed its stalk
its gratitude.
as if to show
ENORMOUS height
it grew to an
a platitude –
with most divine
both day and night
He greeted it
aluminium.
a can of
with water from
and nurtured it
delphinium,
once grew a fine
whose name was Tom
A gardener

# Tout Ensemble

Paula pounds the grand piano,
Vera scrapes the violin,
Percival provides percussion
On an empty biscuit tin,
Connie squeaks the concertina,
Mervyn strums the mandolin.
When you put them all together,
They make one *almighty* din!

# To Be a Bee?

To be a bee, or not to be
A bee, that is the question.
You see, I'm in a quandary.
"To be a bee, or not to be
A bee" is what perplexes me.
Pray, what is your suggestion?
To be a bee, or not to be
A bee, that is the question.

# The Hole Truth

If it takes three men to dig one hole
Two hours and one minute,
How long would six men take to dig
A hole exactly twice as big,
And could you push them in it?

# Grandfather Clock

O Grandfather Clock, dear old Grandfather Clock,
How charming to hear is your tick and your tock.
So upright you stand, day and night in the hall,
Your feet on the ground and your back to the wall.

Although I may grumble
   most mornings at eight,
When you chime, "Hurry up,
   or you're bound to be late!"
I'm grateful to greet you
   at five o'clock when
You chime, "Welcome home,
   nice to see you again!"

I think it is thoughtless
   when relatives speak
And rudely refer to you
   as an antique,
It also seems heartless
   when sometimes they say
You'd fetch a fair price
   at an auction one day.

I know that you're old and can sometimes be slow,
But I hope that they never decide you should go.
How dull life would be if they took you away,
You give me much more than the time of the day.

# Tomorrow I've Given up Hope

I've sailed all the seas in a bathtub,
And climbed all the mountains with rope.
I've flown in the skies with soap in my eyes,
But tomorrow I've given up hope.

I've seen all the world's rarest flowers,
And climbed the uncommonest trees.
I've paddled in ponds and made friends with fronds,
But tomorrow still quite eludes me.

I never have *seen* a tomorrow,
I've never been able to say,
"Tomorrow has come, the bumblebees hum,
Tomorrow's come early today!"